MEL BAY'S GETTING INTO... ROCK GUITAR

by Stephen Delach

CDContents

[1] 1.5	1:19	[19] 2.8	0:13	[37] 4.4	0:22	[55] 6.1	0:16
[2] 1.6	0:14	[20] 2.9	0:13	[38] 4.5	0:12	[56] 6.2	0:13
[3] 1.7	0:17	[21] 2.10	0:21	[39] 4.6	0:20	[57] 6.3	1:00
[4] 1.8	0:14	[22] 2.11	0:27	[40] 4.7	0:15	[58] 6.4	0:13
[5] 1.9	0:11	[23] 2.12	0:15	[41] 4.8	0:25	[59] 6.5	0:13
[6] 1.10	0:13	[24] 2.13	0:28	[42] 4.9	0:20	[60] 6.6	1:10
[7] 1.11	0:10	[25] 2.14	0:22	[43] 4.10	0:20	[61] 25 Pentatonic Licks	2:37
[8] 1.12	0:14	[26] 2.15	0:32	[44] 4.11	0:20	[62] 8.3	0:08
[9] 1.13	0:07	[27] 3.1	0:14	[45] 4.12	0:18	[63] 8.4	0:09
[10] 1.14	0:12	[28] 3.2	0:16	[46] 4.13	0:21	[64] 8.5	0:08
[11] 1.15	0:12	[29] 3.3	0:23	[47] 5.1	0:26	[65] 8.6	0:08
[12] 1.16	0:56	[30] 3.4	0:20	[48] 5.2	0:26	[66] 8.7	0:53
[13] 2.2	0:19	[31] 3.5	0:23	[49] 5.3	0:28	[67] Phrasing	1:11
[14] 2.3	0:21	[32] 3.6	0:16	[50] 5.4	0:24	[68] 25 Blues Licks	3:07
[15] 2.4	0:22	[33] 3.7	0:17	[51] 5.5	0:29	[69] 25 Bends	3:23
[16] 2.5	0:15	[34] 3.8	0:29	[52] 5.6	0:15	[70] Eddie from Etna	1:38
[17] 2.6	0:13	[35] 3.9	0:51	[53] 5.7	0:15	[71] Deli boy Blues	2:53
[18] 2.7	0:21	[36] 4.3	0:21	[54] 5.8	0:27	[72] Funktion	1:49
						[73] Riff Raff	1:42

2 3 4 5 6 7 8 9 0

Visit us on the Web at www.melbay.com — E-mail us at email@melbay.com

Table of Contents

Introduction

Most of the ways guitarists learn are from watching others, listening, reading instructional books etc. We pick up different ideas then try to emulate them. Players have learned from listening and watching each other since the beginning. Learning to play rock guitar is no different.

When you're first starting it's important to realize there are only a handful of scales, chords and techniques that make up rock's underlying foundation. Learning these fundamentals will provide you with a solid structure from which to build upon.

"Getting into Rock" will guide you through the basics that are essential to any rock guitarist, simple but effective. This book is divided into two sections. The first section covers rhythm while the second concentrates on playing lead. When learning any of the examples try to expand on them, Rock is about being creative.

To get a feel for the examples, be sure to go through the book with the CD. Rock is an aural form of music and should be listened to in order to capture its nuances. Use the play-along tracks to improvise over, using the material you've acquired. This book will provide the tools, what you do with them will shape your musical future. Have fun and enjoy.

Steve Delach

Getting Started

When learning any new style of music, a basic knowledge of your instrument is essential. Learning a few fundamentals such as the names of the strings and how to find the notes on the guitar will greatly help in mastering the material in this text. With the information provided in this section you will gain a solid background to build upon, and get down to what it's really about--making music.

Learn Thy Notes

How often have you been jamming with your friends and you start playing a cool lick, and the bass player yells "What Key?" while you're so shaken - trying to count the frets to tell them what number fret to play on. This section shows how you can avoid this embarrassing scenario all together. Sure learning where all the notes on the guitar can be a daunting task, but it doesn't have to be.

First lets look at the names of the six strings starting from the lowest to the highest. (fig. 1)

Figure 1

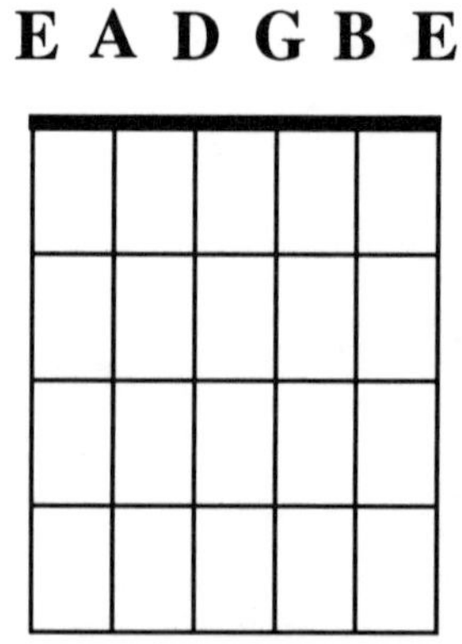

E A D G B E

In music there are 7 diatonic notes (no sharps or flats).

A B C D E F G

To break down the neck and find all the diatonic notes let's use just one string at a time.

1. Only use your first finger for this entire exercise (the idea is to identify where the notes are on the fretboard).

2. Start with the low E string, play and say the name of each note up the string. For example the notes would be as follows **E, F, G, A, B, C, D, E** repeat this process on the next five strings. The notes will always follow alphabetically.

3. Only go up to the 12 fret (after the 12 fret all the notes repeat up an octave higher in pitch)

4. **B** to **C** and **E** to **F** have 1/2 steps between them, all other notes will be in whole steps

When concentrating on one string at a time you will be able to visualize the fretboard in a clearer fashion. Start with one string a week until you can identify the notes on all six. This knowledge will greatly speed up the learning process and impress your friends. Here, they are laid out.

Single String Notes

6th String E

5th String A

4th String D

3rd String G

2nd String B

1st String E

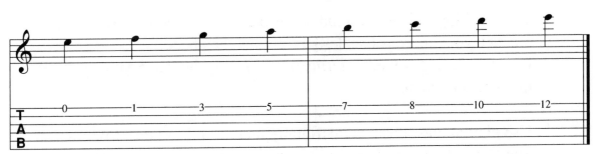

To sharp (♯) a note - move up a 1/2 step from the note you're on.

To flat (♭) a note - move down a 1/2 step from the note you're on.

Tips to Make the Most of Your Practice / Playing Time

Listening

An important aspect of learning rock guitar is listening. When you listen to other players you pick up different ideas, techniques, but mainly inspiration. Finding a player you like and emulating his tone or feel is not a bad thing. Take an idea and make it your own

Practicing

1. When you learn any new material be sure to play it slowly to ensure accuracy. This will help when trying to play faster.

2. Use repetition-keep repeating a lick or chord that is giving you trouble. I guarantee that after five minutes you'll have a pretty good handle on it.

Playing

1. A good thing to keep in mind when playing is--nothing. You want to practice your chords or scales so well that they become second nature. If your playing sounds sterile it's probably because you're think-ing way too much.

2. Use play-alongs, these are definitely a Godsend. A solid rhythm sec-tion to practice over is essential for developing good timing as well as learning how to improvise and construct solos. Be sure to check out the play-a-long tracks at the end of the book.

Rhythm Guitar

A crucial part of rock guitar is rhythm. If you're like me the first thing you did when you got your first guitar was tried to play lead. But, what can really make a tune interesting is the rhythmic aspect of it. Your job as a rock guitarist is to lock in with the rhythm section (the drums and bass). The importance of the rhythm section as a whole is to hold everything together, create a cushion for the vocalist or soloist. In this first section we'll explore some different facets of rhythm guitar.

The Power Chord

The power chord has been in existence since the beginning of rock. Without it we would all sound like Jewel (not that there's anything wrong with that) but you get the picture. Made up of just 2 notes (root and 5th) the power chord can produce a really big sound with little effort. Figure 1.A – 1.C show different fingerings using open strings. While figures 1.D – 1.F show movable shapes. The bottom note is the root (where a chord or scale gets its name).

Open Position Power Chords

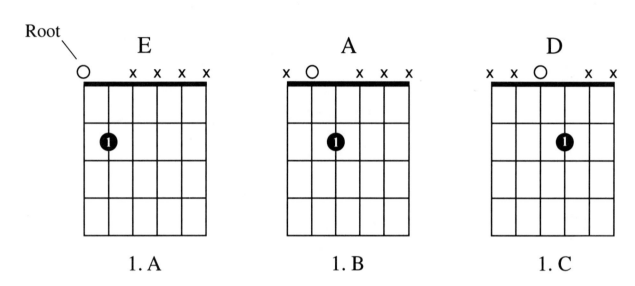

Movable Power Chords

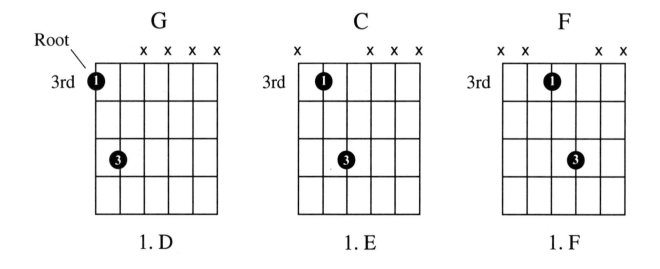

Progressions

Here are some progressions to get you moving around (ex. 1.1 - 1.5), see whether you can play them in different areas of the neck. Remember the lowest note in the power chord is the root-where the chord gets its name. Pay close attention to example 1.5, it's a twelve bar blues progression. This progression is used in all areas of rock, and it makes for a good vehicle to jam on. We'll be expanding upon it throughout the book.

Ex. 1.1

Ex. 1.2

Ex. 1.3

Ex. 1.4

Twelve Bar Blues

Ex. 1.5

Rhythms

Rhythms are an integral part of rock guitar. Examples 1.6 - 1.10 show mixed rhythms using only the open E power chord. You can produce a lot of rhythmic variety from one simple chord.

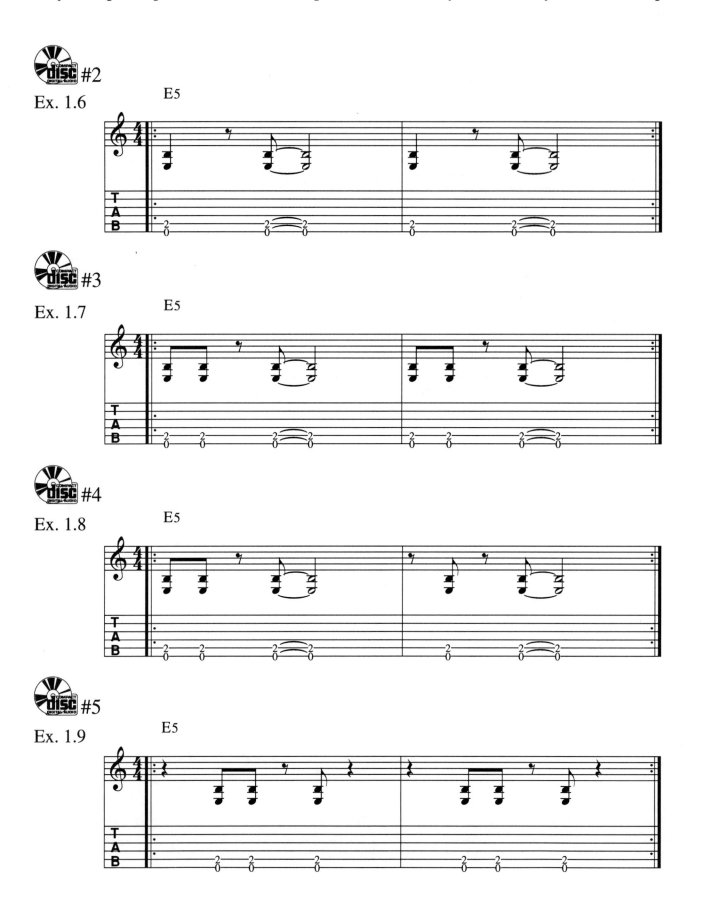

Ex. 1.10

Power Chord Add Ons

Some players will double the 5th in a power chord (fig. 1. G). Hendrix used this technique in "The Wind Cries Mary."

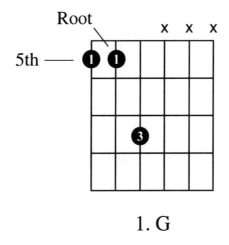

1. G

Ex. 1.11

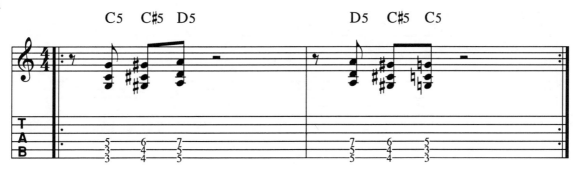

Another popular note you can add to the power chord is the 9th (fig. 1.I - 1.J). Dave Mathews and The Police use this sound exclusively.

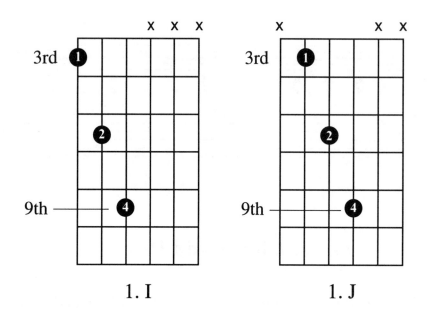

1. I   1. J

 #8

Ex. 1.12

 #9

Ex. 1.13

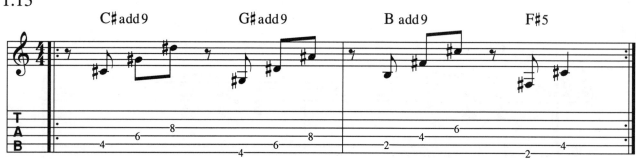

Adding notes to the E power chord will give it more of a bluesy sound as in examples 1.14 and 1.15. Listen to the CD to get a feel for the rhythm.

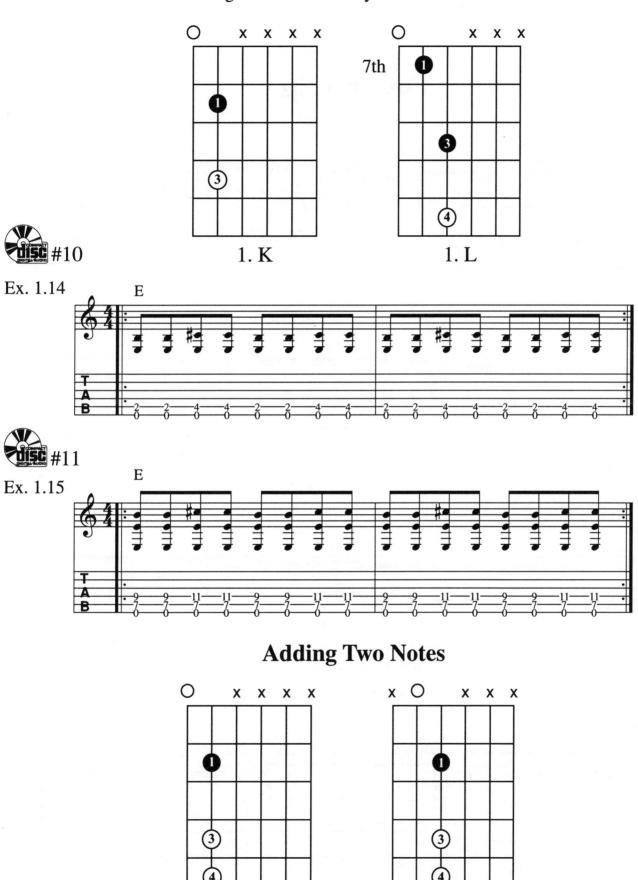

#10

Ex. 1.14

#11

Ex. 1.15

Adding Two Notes

1. M   1. N

Here's a twelve bar blues in E using this type of chord movement.

#12

Power Trip

Ex. 1.16

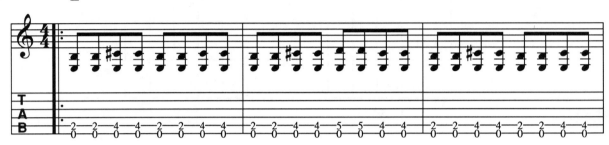

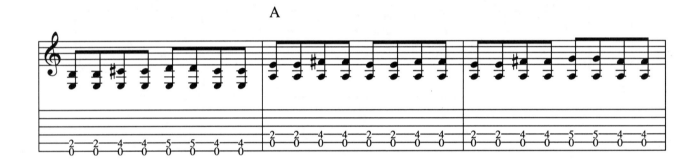

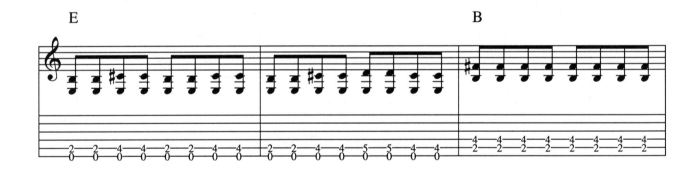

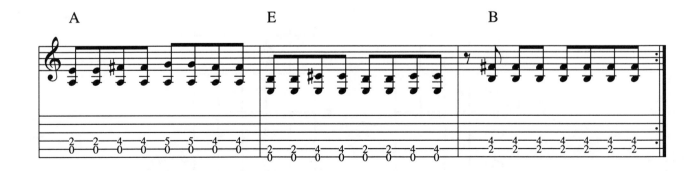

Intervals

You have probably played intervals before without ever realizing what they were called. In fact, we've already played an interval last chapter, the power chord. Just two notes but intervals have created countless classic guitar licks. In this section we'll look at some common intervals found in rock.

What is an Interval?

If you've ever been confused about what a 5th or a root is then this section will help clear it up. Here's a simple way of creating intervals (the distance between two notes). First lets start with the C major scale. This scale is the building block of music (fig. 2).

Figure 2

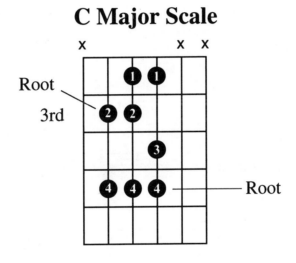

Ex. 2.1

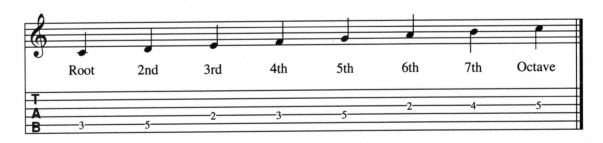

There are 7 notes in this scale plus the octave = 8 notes. Starting from C the first note of the scale is called the root. From C to D is a 2nd, from C to E is a 3rd, C to F is a 4th, etc. Every time you go up a note from C (the root) this note will get a number. So what's this have to do with rock? Knowing how to communicate with other musicians is key in expressing your musical ideas for tunes, rhythms etc. This can also avoid many band fights.

Major and Minor 3rds

To make a minor 3rd, flat the E. Learn to visualize the shapes and hear the sound.

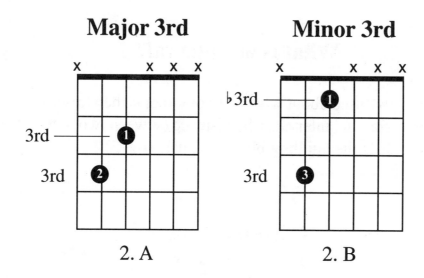

Major 3rd

Minor 3rd

2. A   2. B

 #13

Ex. 2.2

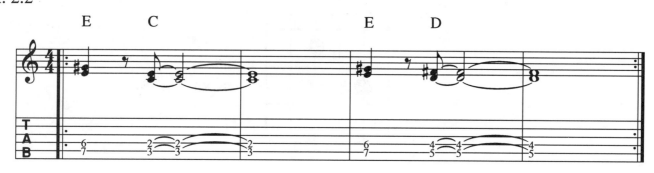

 #14

Ex. 2.3

18

Some players will raise the third up an octave.

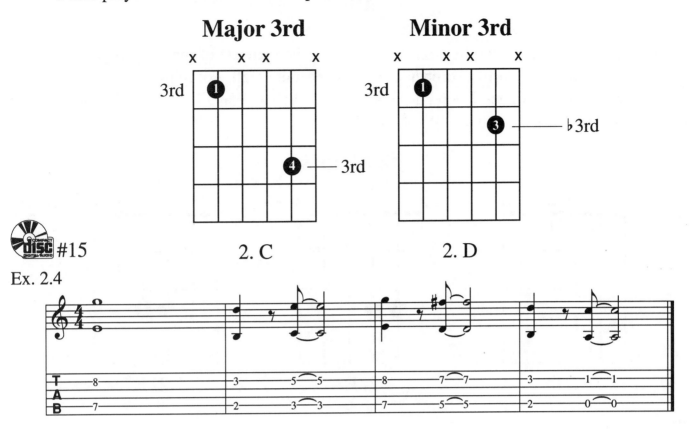

Major 3rd   **Minor 3rd**

2. C   2. D

#15

Ex. 2.4

You can also use the open G string in combination with 3rds. The Beatles used this technique in "Blackbird."

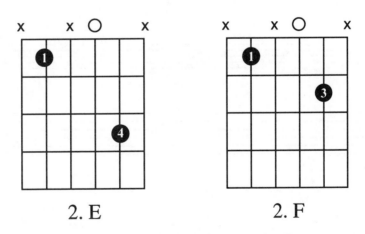

2. E   2. F

This example would make a good ending for a tune in G.

#16

Ex. 2.5

4ths

4ths can produce everything from roots rock to the heaviest of metal. The guitars bottom four strings are tuned in fourths, so open strings work quite well, not to mention you can easily grab them with just one finger. Deep Purple's "Smoke On The Water" is one of the most famous rock tunes that uses 4ths.

4th Shapes

2. G   2. H   2. I

 #17

Key of G Minor

Ex. 2.6

 #18

Key of A Minor

Ex. 2.7

Key of A or A Minor

 #19

Ex. 2.8

♭5

Ah, the ♭5, without this interval we would not have metal.

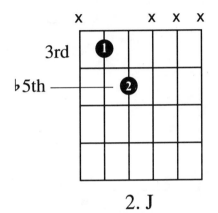

2. J

 #20

Ex. 2.9

Key of C Minor

 #21

Key of E Minor

Ex. 2.10

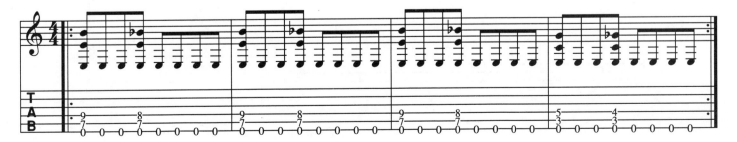

6ths

This sound can be heard in more of the blues and soulful side of rock. Early Rolling Stones and The Black Crowe's have used this sound extensively.

6th Shapes

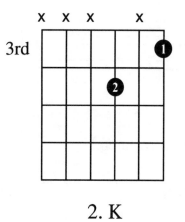

2. K   2. L

#22

Ex. 2.11

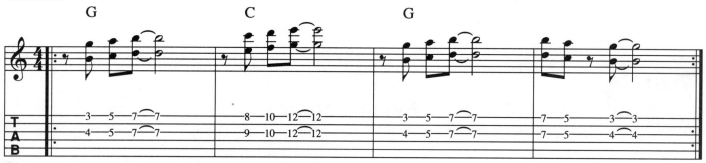

#23

Ex. 2.12

Octaves

Though long associated with jazzers. Rock musicians such as Jimi Hendrix and Stevie Ray Vaughan have used octaves as part of their musical arsenal.

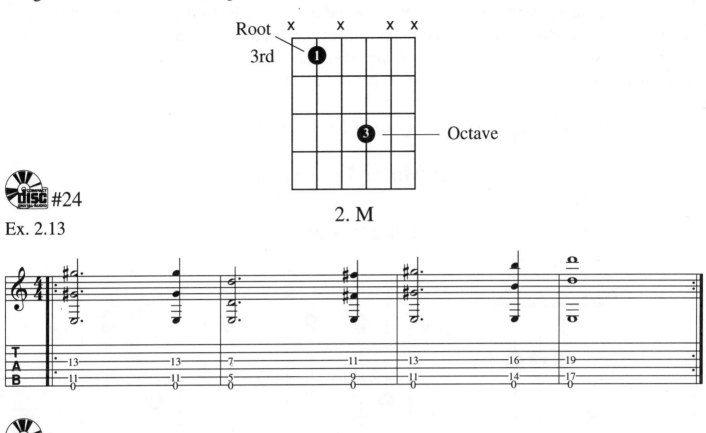

 #24

Ex. 2.13

 #25

Ex. 2.14

 #26

Ex. 2.15

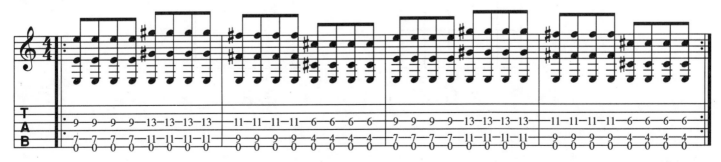

Inversions

Watch any professional play rhythm guitar and I highly doubt you'll see many barre chords being played. Players tend to use 3, or 4 note inversions of chords (a different order of playing the notes in a chord). When you need a different flavor other than power chord, inversions can't be beat. They also work great when playing with other guitarists to fill out a rhythm part. To get a more mature sound with a lot less effort, inversions are the way to go.

Here are some frequently used inversions for **A Major.**

A Major Inversions

Middle Strings

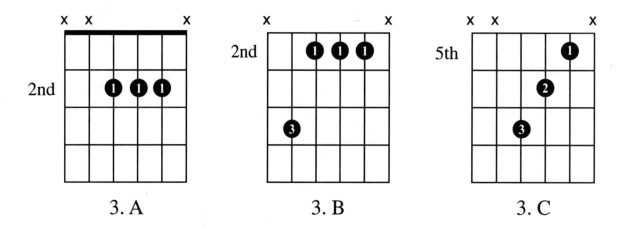

3. A   3. B   3. C

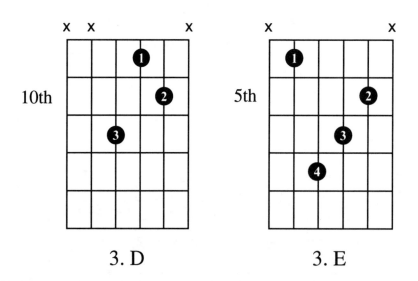

3. D   3. E

24

A Major Inversions

Top Strings

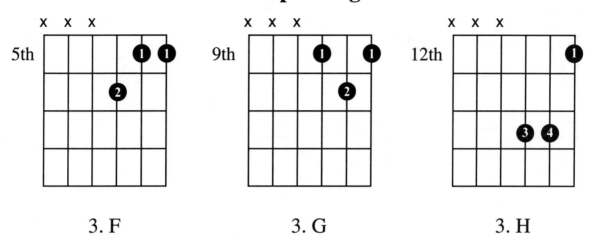

3. F   3. G   3. H

Check out the examples for some different uses. Expand upon them and make them your own.

 #27

Ex. 3.1

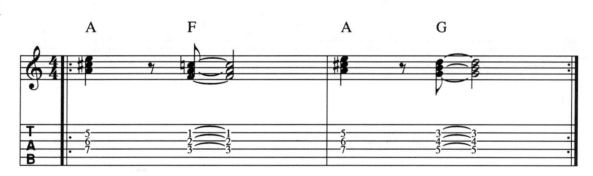

 #28

Ex. 3.2

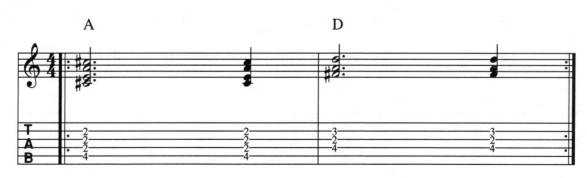

25

#29

Ex. 3.3

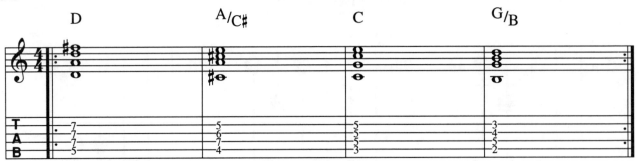

 #30

Ex. 3.4

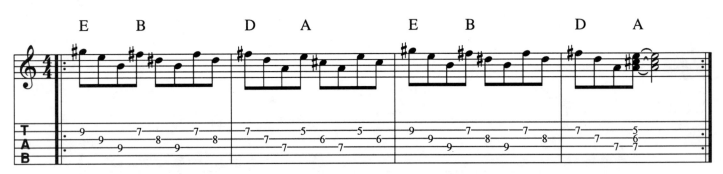

 #31

Ex. 3.5

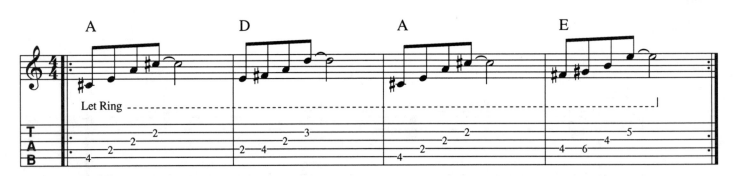

A Minor Inversions

Middle Strings

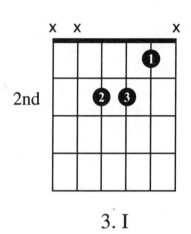

3. I

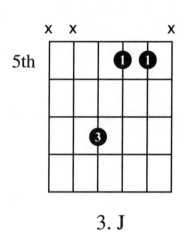

3. J

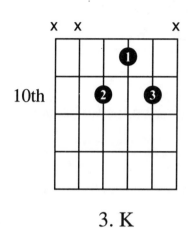

3. K

Top Strings

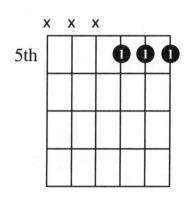

3. L

3. M

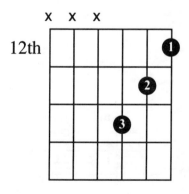

3. N

#32

Ex. 3.6

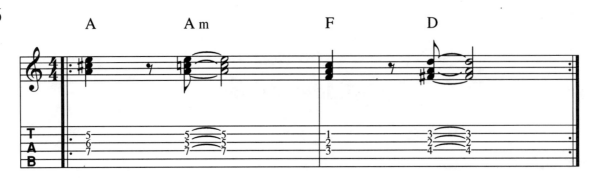

Playing on the up beats produces this Police inspired example.

 #33

Ex. 3.7

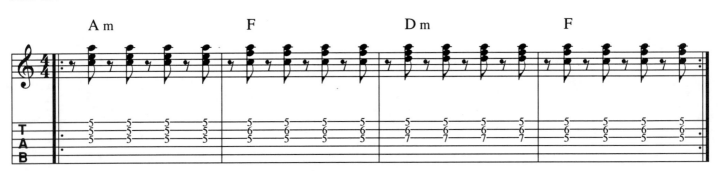

 #34

Ex. 3.8

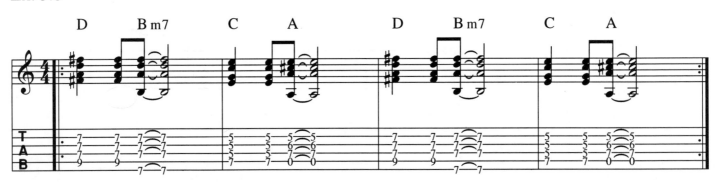

Finally, here's a short piece illustrating how to use inversions over a simple chord progression.

Dude......Etude

Ex. 3.9

29

Riffs

Along with power chords, intervals and inversions another key ingredient of rock rhythm guitar are riffs. Riffs are not chords but scale based playing, usually played off the lower strings to create a more driving rhythm part. With riffs you can achieve a heavier sound or provide a catchy hook to a song. Led Zeppelin and Black Sabbath are some of the great riff oriented bands.

The Blues Scale

To get us started lets look at an E blues scale in two different positions. We'll concentrate on only the bottom three strings using just one octave (fig. 4.A - 4.B). In the next section of the book we'll discuss how to use the blues scale in your lead playing.

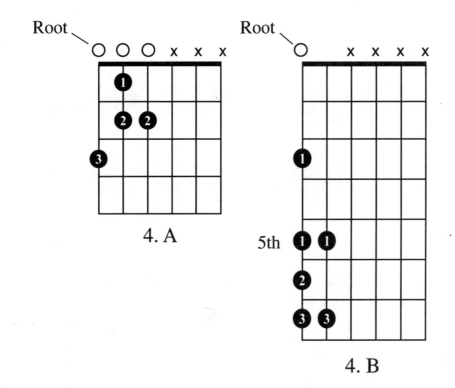

4. A

4. B

E Blues Scale
(First Position)

Ex. 4.1

E Blues Scale
(Second Position)

Ex. 4.2

Riffs for the E The Blues Scale

 #36

Ex. 4.3

You can play the same lick using a different position for a tighter sound.

 #37

Ex. 4.4

#38

Ex. 4.5

 #39

Ex. 4.6

 #40

Ex. 4.7

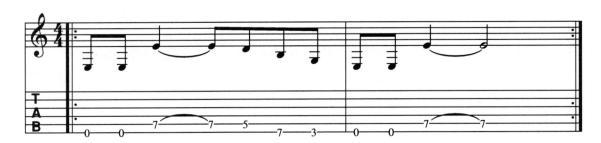

 #41

Ex. 4.8

You can use riffs in any key or with any scale. Here are some using the **A Blues Scale.**

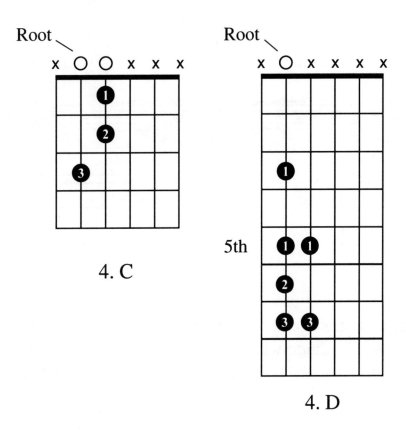

4. C

4. D

Riffs for the A The Blues Scale

 #42

Ex. 4.9

 #43

Ex. 4.10

#44

Ex. 4.11

Drop D

Another technique that has been known to conjure up some bodacious riffs is the drop D tuning. Simply tune your low E string a whole step lower to D, the other strings remain in standard tuning. Everyone from Van Halen to the 90's grunge movement has used the drop D tuning.

 #45

Ex. 4.12

 #46

Ex. 4.13

Tricks of the Trade

Students often tell me they have their first position chords down, but what can they do with them to make their playing more interesting? In this section we'll discuss a few "tricks of the trade" using first position chords.

I have always been a firm believer in watching the way others play. Most method books will tell you to play an A chord with three fingers, but playing an A chord with just your first finger (fig. 5.A) is how Pete Townsend and Keith Richards would play it, and that's the seal of approval. "Keep things simple" is a good motto to follow in rock music.

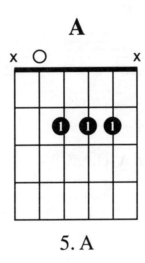

5. A

To break out of mundane strumming patterns, arpeggiating chords is a good way to add some momentum to a rhythm part (ex 5.1)

 #47

Ex. 5.1

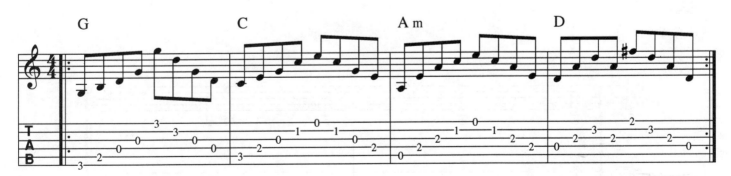

35

Chord Movement

Moving one note inside a G chord can add a variety of tonal colors (ex. 5.2).

 #48

Ex. 5.2

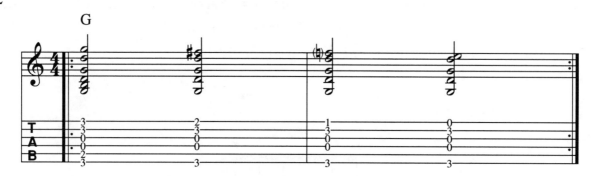

Here are some examples using an **A** chord.

 #49

Ex. 5.3

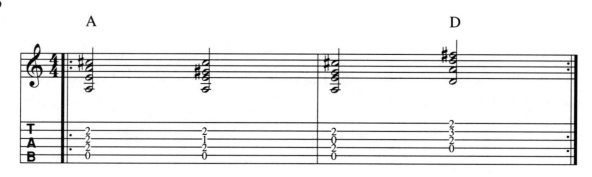

 #50

Ex. 5.4

D shape

Taking one shape and moving it around the neck will create a lot of different sounds (ex. 5.5). This technique was really popular in the 70's arena rock era.

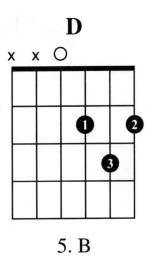

5. B

 #51

Ex. 5.5

A helpful way of learning and remembering a new chord is through recognition. A player might use the same chord in many of his or her tunes. You can benefit from being able to identify the chord with that player. Even if you don't know the name of it, visualize the shape and hear the sound. Don't worry, you can always learn the names of chords later. This is how it's been done since the beginning.

D/F♯ - The "Clapton Chord"

D/F♯ is a D chord with an F♯ in the bass and has been played in an abundance of Eric Clapton tunes. It's also made its way into quite a few Beatles and Zeppelin tunes as well. Here are some examples demonstrating the D/F♯.

D/F♯   **(Movable Shape)**

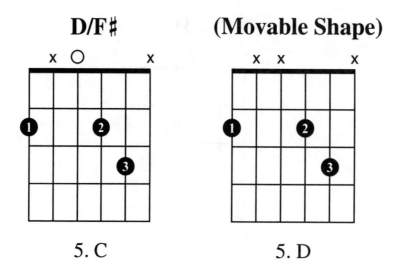

5. C   5. D

 #52

Ex. 5.6

 #53

Ex. 5.7

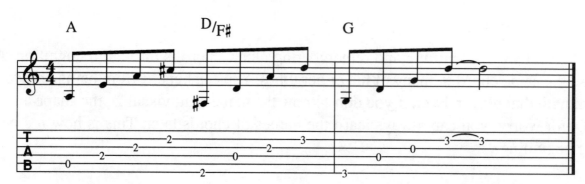

38

Ex. 5.8

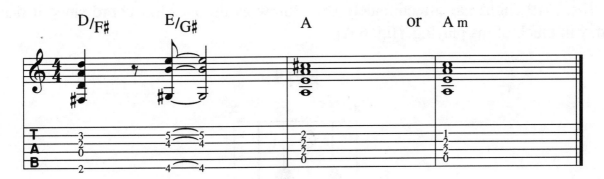

E7♯9

So far we've covered a lot of material found in rock rhythm. In this section we'll look at a few other chords that have made their way into the rock repertoire.

The E7♯9 chord has affectionately been know as the Hendrix chord since it has been a mainstay in much of his playing. (fig. 6.A)

E7♯9

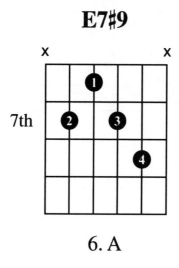

6. A

E7♯9 Examples

#55

Ex. 6.1

#56

Ex. 6.2

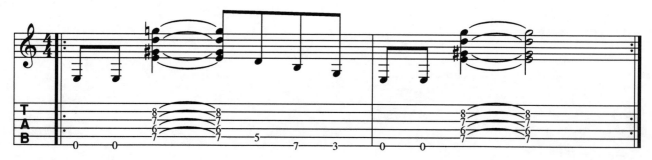

Here's a short etude utilizing the 7#9 chord over a twelve bar blues.

Jerky

Ex. 6.3

The Funky Side of Rock

The funk rock movement credited mainly to the Red Hot Chili Peppers has also popularized the 7#9 chord.

The rhythm for this type of playing requires a very relaxed picking hand. Listen to the CD to hear how the examples should be played.

 #58

Ex. 6.4

 #59

Ex. 6.5

Another chord that has been frequently used in the funk rock genre is the 9th.

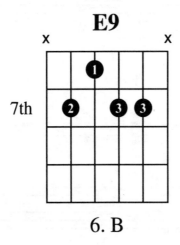

6. B

When learning any new style or technique, listening is just as important as actually playing and practicing. Keep an open ear. Be creative with the techniques and examples you have learned.

And finally another etude using 9th and 7#9 chords, entitled "Funk in A."

Funk in A

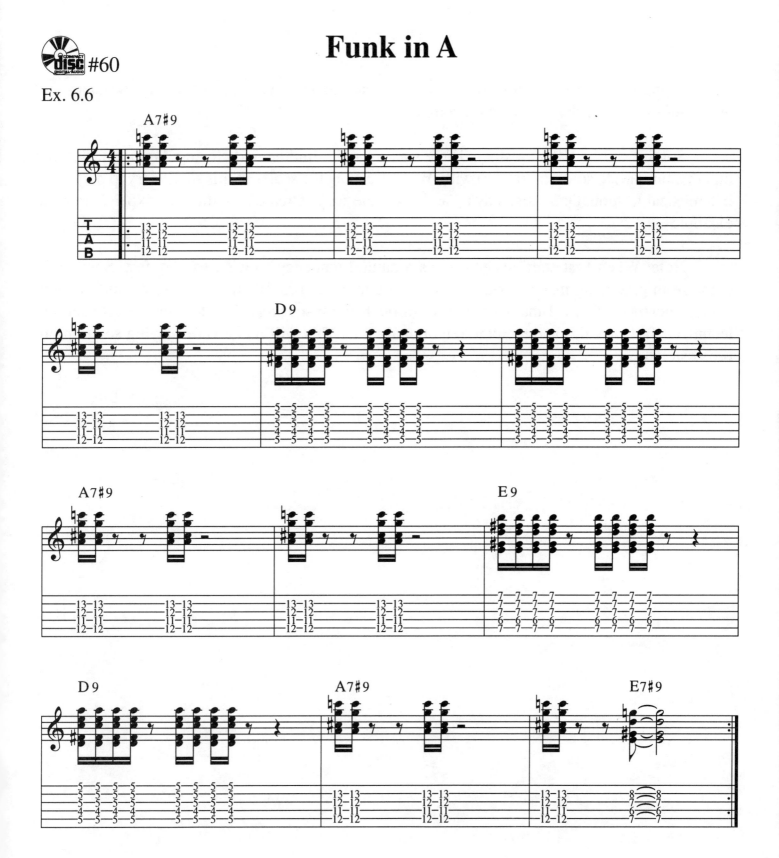

Lead Introduction

In the second part of this book entitled "Lead Guitar," we'll put to use a few scales and techniques that have defined the rock sound.

Soloing is like telling a story. There's an opening, middle and closing. We use scales and other techniques to solo (improvise) with. When learning the scales in this section try to play them in a musical fashion. Don't just play up and down the scale. Create melodies and expand upon the examples.

Note; When first starting out there's a natural tendency to want to play fast. Speed will come from practicing material slowly. But, more important is the melodic (emotional) element players possess. It's as if they are singing through the instrument. Try to balance between the technical (fast playing) and melodic (emotional) side. This will make your playing sound more professional.

Pentatonics

As with the power chord, without the pentatonic scale rock would not exist. Made up of five notes (R, ♭3, 4, 5, ♭7) the pentatonic originated from Chinese music and has somehow managed to become rock's most popular scale. To get us started with this scale let's break it up into two sections (ex. 7.A - 7.B). Learning a scale this way will help you visualize it clearer. Another element to mastering the pentatonic; rock guitarists mostly use their first and third fingers to play this scale. Experiment playing the scale with different fingerings.

A Minor Pentatonic

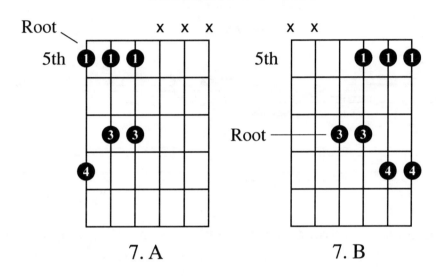

7. A   7. B

Ex. 7.1

Ex. 7.2

A Minor Pentatonic
(Full Scale)

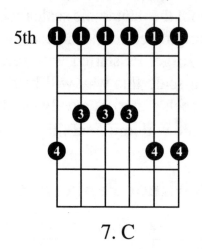

7. C

Ex. 7.3

To use the minor pentatonic over a major sounding progression play the minor pentatonic down a minor 3rd. For example, if playing in C use an A minor pentatonic to solo with. The Allman Brothers and Grateful Dead used this sound a great deal.

Here are a few more ways of fingering an **A Minor pentatonic** scale. (ex. 7.D and 7.E) These positions will help break you out of the traditional "box" shapes and get you moving more along the neck. Watch any of the greats play from Eddie Van Halen to Eric Clapton to Stevie Ray; they all play up and down the neck in addition to the box shape.

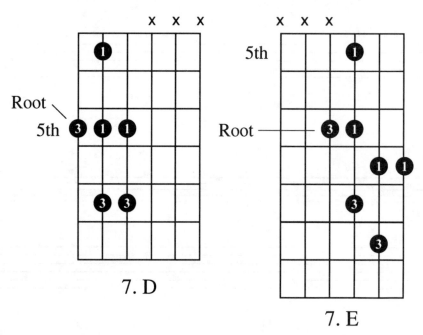

7. D

7. E

Ex. 7.4

Ex. 7.5

A Minor Pentatonic
(Full Scale Up the Neck)

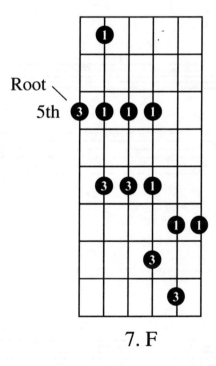

7. F

Ex. 7.6

47

This is the second most common position rock players use for the **A Minor Pentatonic.**

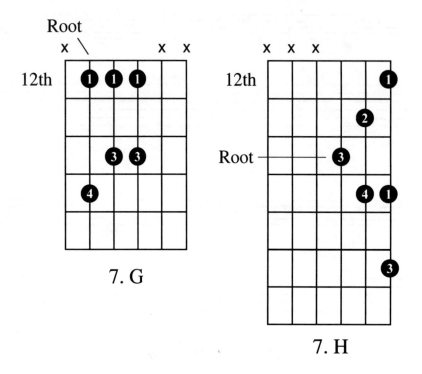

7. G

7. H

Ex. 7.7

Ex. 7.8

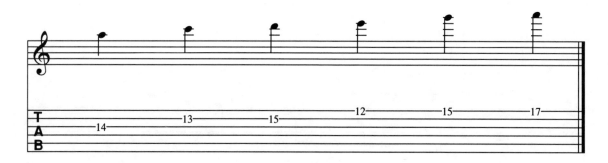

A Minor Pentatonic
(Full Scale)

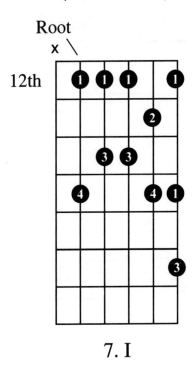

7. I

Ex. 7.9

Here are some patterns using the A minor pentatonic scale.

Ex. 7.10

Ala Jimmy Page

Ex. 7.11

Ex. 7.12

Ex. 7.13

Ex. 7.14

25 Pentatonic Licks

Finally, here are 25 licks using the A minor pentatonic. Learning licks will help you when improvising and constructing solos. You can play them over any A chord.

Ex. 7.15

Ex. 7.16

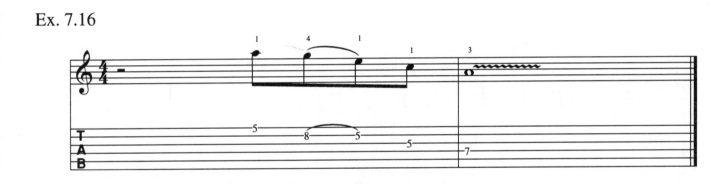

Ex. 7.17

Ex. 7.18

Two notes can say a lot, just listen to B.B. King and Carlos Santana.

Ex. 7.19

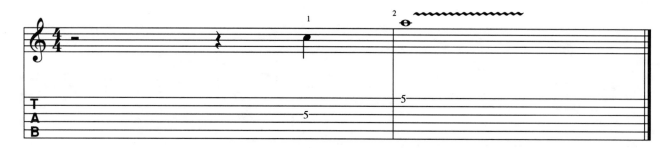

Ex. 7.20

Here is a Chuck Berry inspired riff.

Ex. 7.21

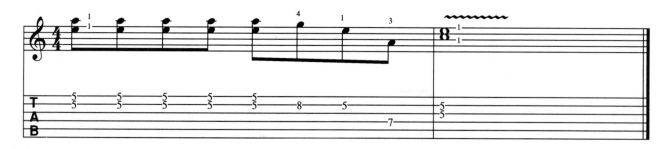

Ex. 7.22

Ex. 7.23

Ex. 7.24

Ex. 7.25

Ex. 7.26

Ex. 7.27

Ex. 7.28

Ex. 7.29

Here is a very popular blues lick.

Ex. 7.30

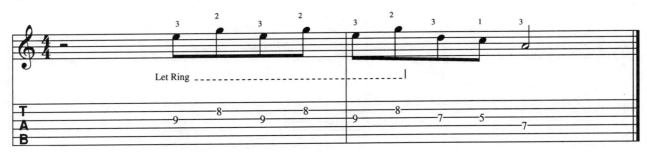

Ex. 7.31

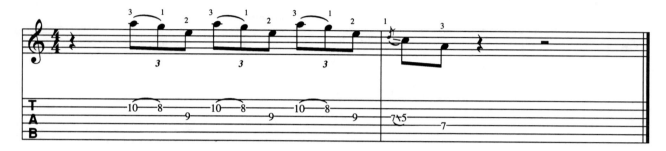

Using a Different Position

Ex. 7.32

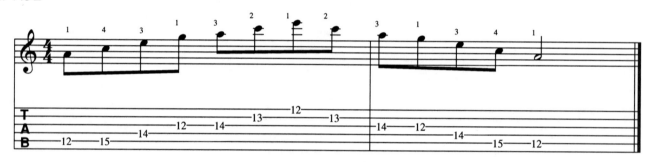

Ex. 7.33

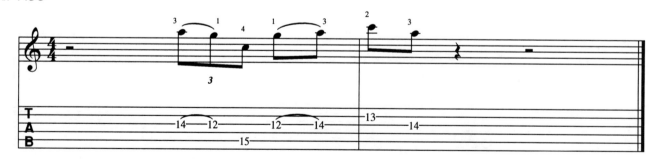

Ex. 7.34

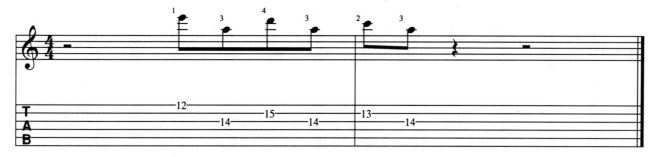

Ex. 7.35

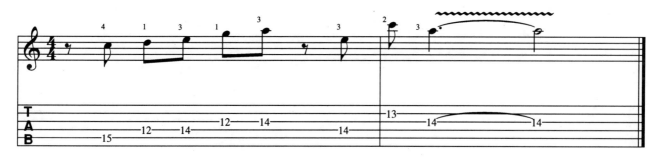

Ex. 7.36

Ex. 7.37

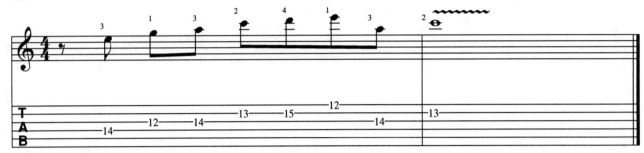

Ex. 7.38

Ex. 7.39

Double Stops

When outlining the A minor pentatonic scale with intervals you will produce major 3rds, 4ths and 5ths (fig. 8.A – 8.H). A popular term for this is called "double stops." Double stops can add variety and movement to a solo. Play the highlighted notes together.

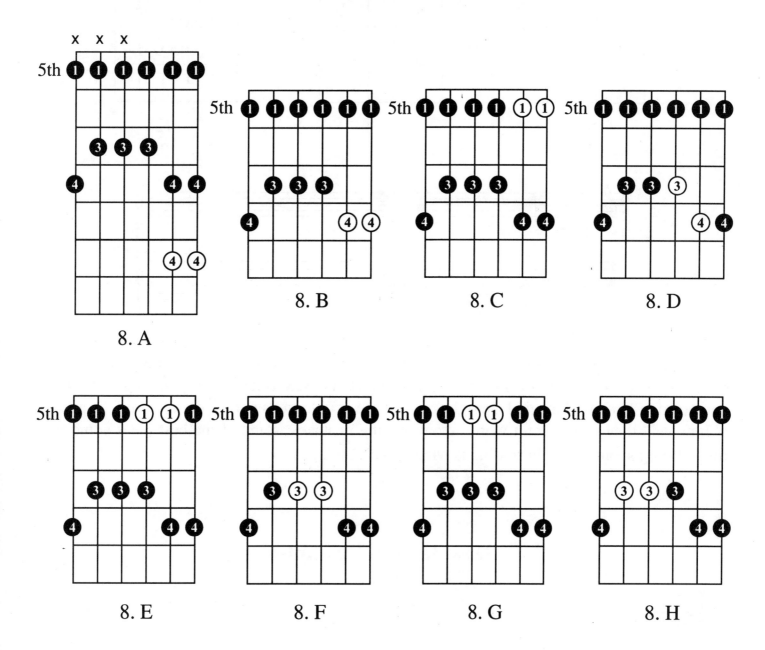

8. A

8. B

8. C

8. D

8. E

8. F

8. G

8. H

Ex. 8.1

59

Players also add 3rds within this shape.

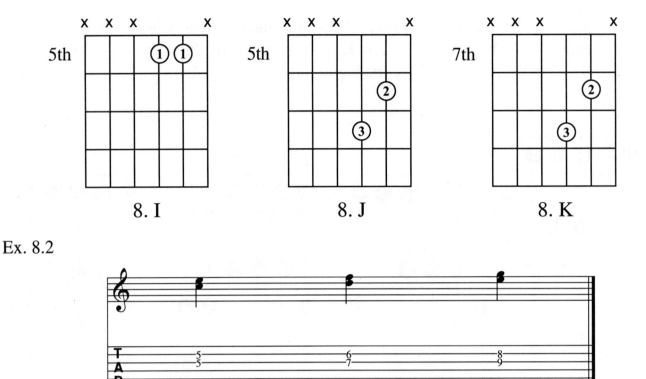

Ex. 8.2

Double stops are also a good tool for faking your way through a song. This is not cheating but actually great ear training. Learn to rely on your ears. Next time you're jamming with a band, and you don't know a tune find the right key and use double stops to play out of. You'll be amazed at how well they work. Don't worry about making mistakes; some of the best ideas come from them. Being spontaneous in soloing is what make's rock fun.

Double Stop Examples

#62

Ex. 8.3

#63

Ex. 8.4

 #64

Ex. 8.5

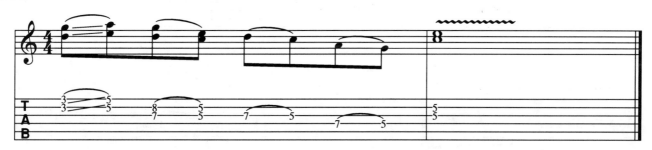

 #65

Ex. 8.6

Finally, a short etude putting double stops to use.

Jennifer's Dilemma

Ex. 8.7

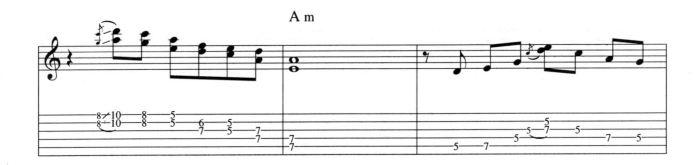

The Blues Scale

The Blues scale is a six note scale. Add one note, the ♭5 to the pentatonic scale and you have the blues scale (R, ♭3, 4, ♭5, 5, ♭7). Besides the pentatonic, the blues scale is rock's second most popular scale. It sounds great over all kinds of rock progressions, but treat the ♭5 with care. If you land on this note it will sound bad, use it in passing. Here are some different fingerings for the blues scale (fig. 9.A - 9.B). Again we'll start with one section of the scale to aid in the learning process.

The Blues Scale

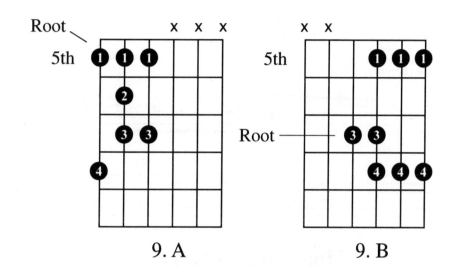

9. A   9. B

Ex. 9.1

Ex. 9.2

A Blues Scale
(Full Scale)

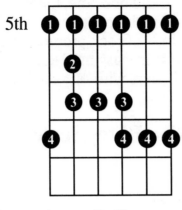

9. C

Ex. 9.3

(More Fingerings)

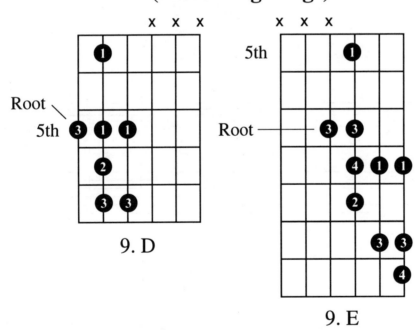

9. D

9. E

Ex. 9.4

Ex. 9.5

A Blues Scale
(Full Scale Up the Neck)

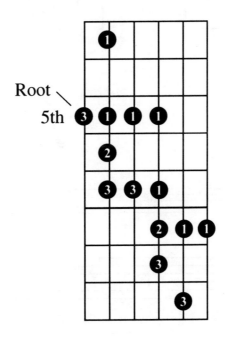

Ex. 9.6

Different position for the **A Blues Scale**.

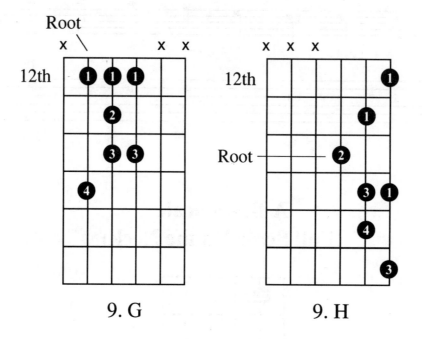

9. G   9. H

Ex. 9.7

Ex. 9.8

A Blues Scale
(Full Scale)

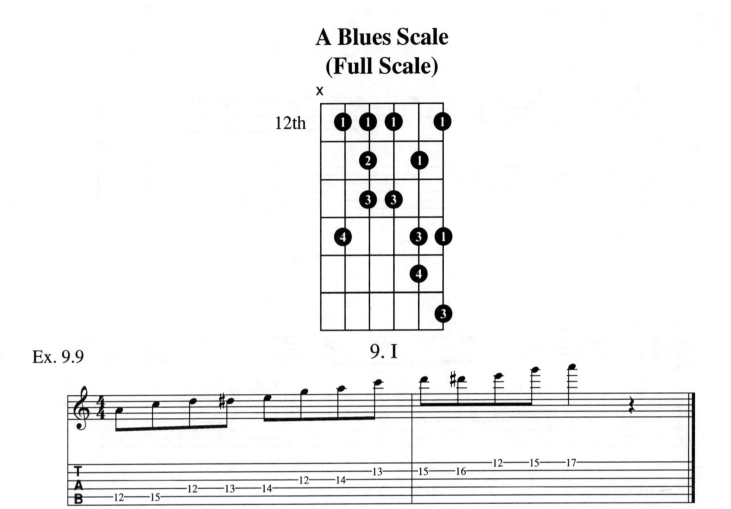

9. I

Ex. 9.9

Phrasing

Phrasing can be thought of as how we communicate through our instrument. When we speak our words come out slow, fast, soft, loud (peaks and valleys), your playing should have a flowing sense to it; not just a bunch of rambling. Some players are on top of the beat or slightly behind, this is what can give you a distinct personality on the instrument. It's what sets players apart.

In this section we'll look at different beats to come in on (ways to phrase your notes) using the blues scale (ex. 9.10 - 9.17). You can get a lot of mileage out of using this simple technique. Listen to the CD to hear this concept put to use. Again we'll use a twelve bar blues progression in A for the backing tracks.

#67

Ex. 9.10   *A Blues Scale*

Ex. 9.11

Ex. 9.12

Ex. 9.13

Ex. 9.14

Ex. 9.15

Ex. 9.16

Ex. 9.17

25 Blues Licks

Here are 25 licks to help get you acquainted with the blues scale.

Ex. 9.18

Ex. 9.19

Ex. 9.20

Ex. 9.21

Ex. 9.22

Ex. 9.23

Ex. 9.24

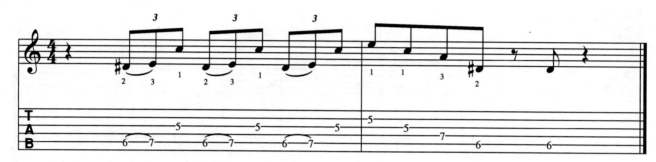

Ex. 9.25

Ex. 9.26

Ex. 9.27

Ex. 9.28

Ex. 9.29

Ex. 9.30

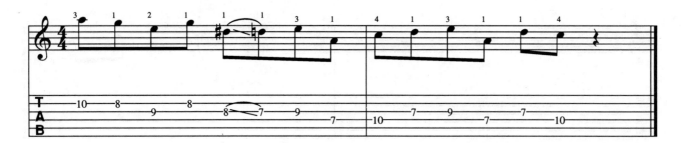

Ex. 9.31

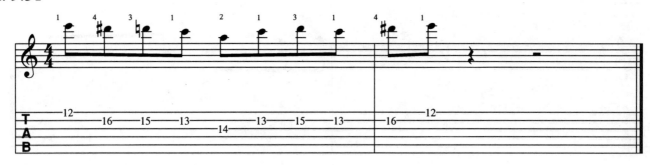

Ex. 9.32

Ex. 9.33

Ex. 9.34

Ex. 9.35

75

Ex. 9.36

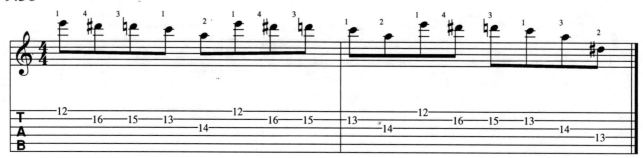

Ex. 9.37

Ex. 9.38

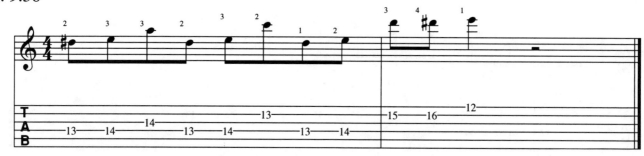

Ex. 9.39

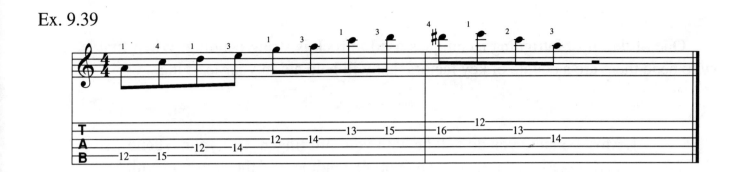

Ex. 9.40

Ex. 9.41

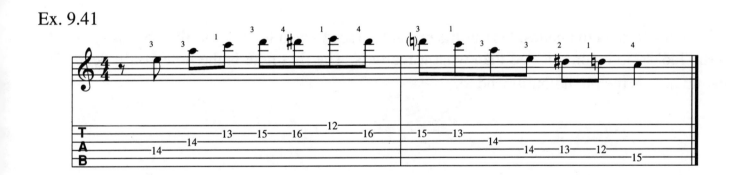

Ex. 9.42

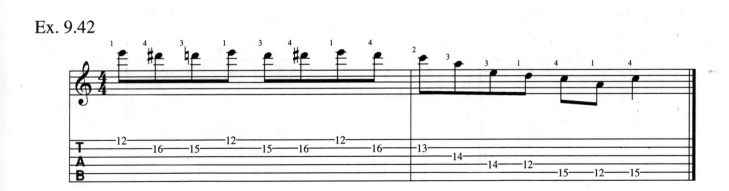

Bends

One of the most intriguing techniques used in rock is string bending. When first learning how to bend there are a couple of key factors that will help aid in your learning.

1. Most bending you do will be with your 3rd finger. Use your 1st and 2nd fingers on the same string you're bending, and then push up with all three fingers. Try to keep your fingers arched. If stretched out straight, your fingers will be in pain. You can also bend using your first finger. Most first finger bends usually bend toward the ground.

2. You should strive to bend to the correct pitch you're aiming for. Before you bend the string play the note you're trying to match, then bend the string.

3. Watching how other players bend is just as important as listening. Taking a few minutes a day on bends will greatly increase your ability to master this technique.

While there are plenty of possibilities we'll concentrate on bending in whole steps and half steps.

How to read the bends. One of the obstacles faced when learning to read bends is that the music looks more complicated than what it really is. The first note is the note you'll bend. The second note is the pitch you'll bend to.

Whole Step Bend

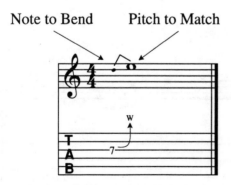

Half Step Bend

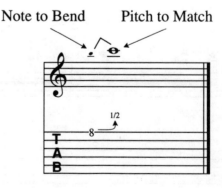

The highlighted notes are good notes to bend in the **A Minor Pentatonic**.

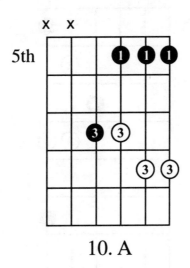

10. A

Whole Step Bends

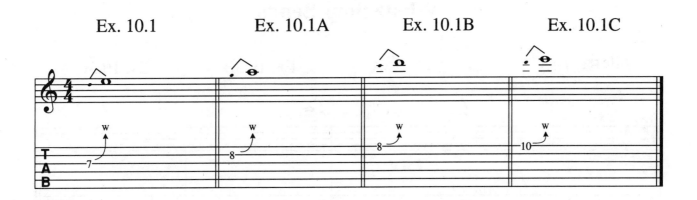

Ex. 10.1   Ex. 10.1A   Ex. 10.1B   Ex. 10.1C

Half Step Bends

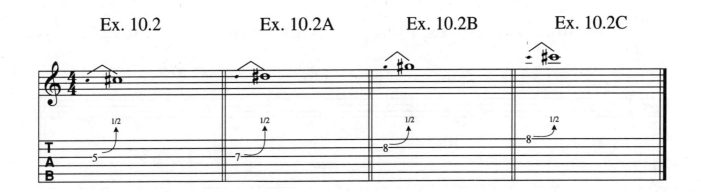

Ex. 10.2   Ex. 10.2A   Ex. 10.2B   Ex. 10.2C

Good notes to bend in a different position of the **A Minor Pentatonic.**

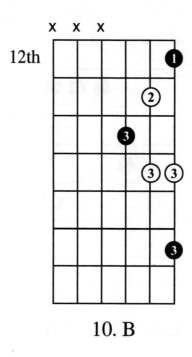

10. B

Whole Step Bends

Ex. 10.3   Ex. 10.3A   Ex. 10.3B   Ex. 10.3C

Half Step Bends

Ex. 10.4   Ex. 10.4A   Ex. 10.4B   Ex. 10.4C

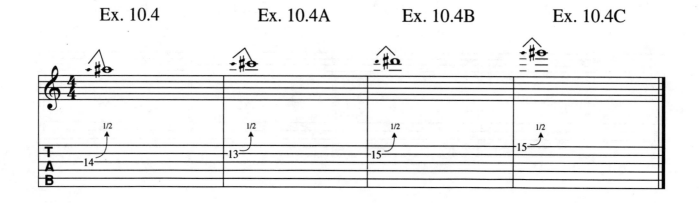

25 Bending Examples

Ex. 10.5

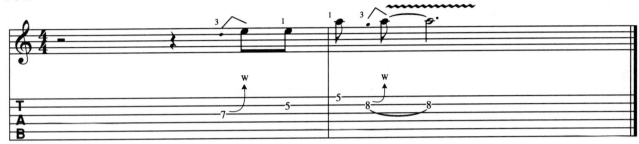

Ex. 10.6

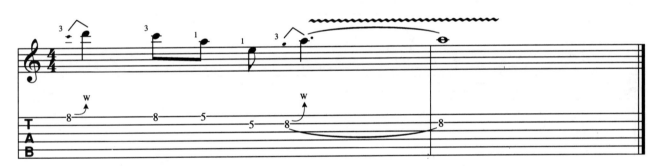

Ex. 10.7

Ex. 10.8

Ex. 10.9

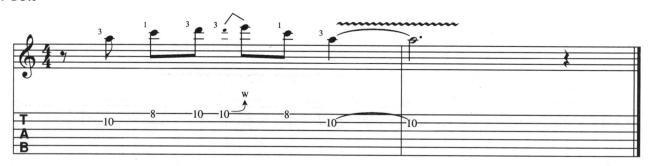

Ex. 10.10

Ex. 10.11

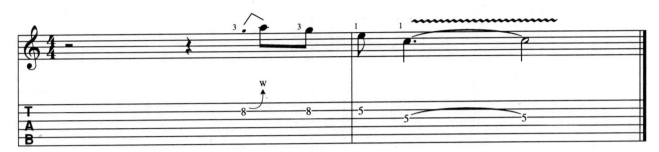

Ex. 10.12

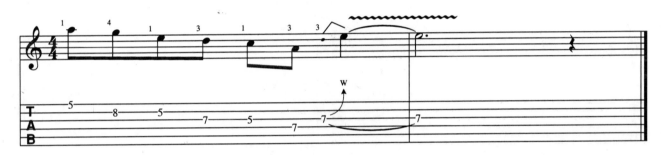

Ex. 10.13

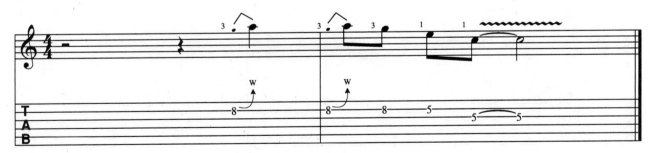

83

Ex. 10.14

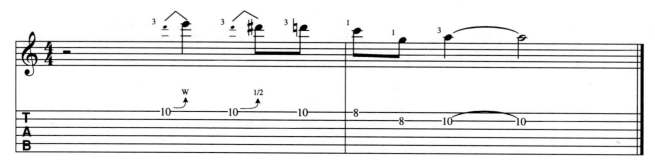

Ex. 10.15

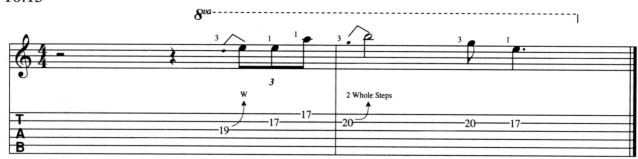

Ex. 10.16

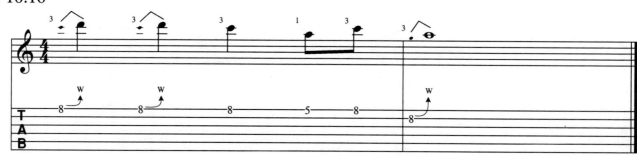

Ex. 10.17

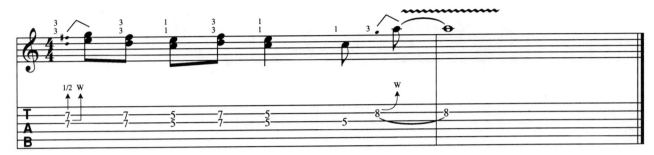

Ex. 10.18

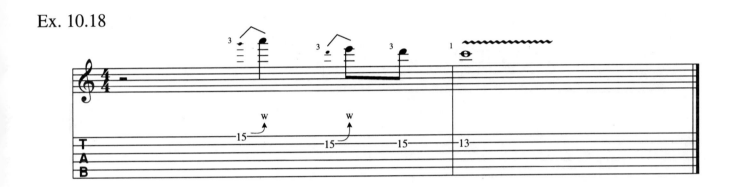

Ex. 10.19

Ex. 10.20

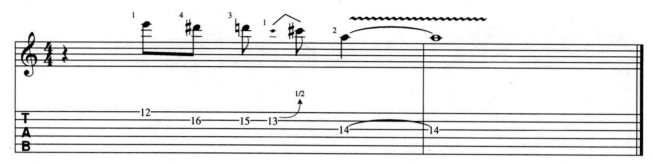

Ex. 10.21

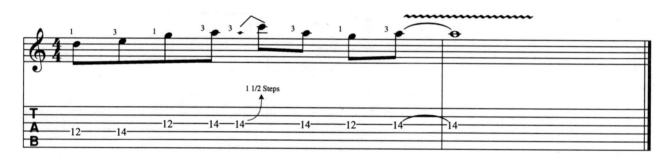

Ex. 10.22

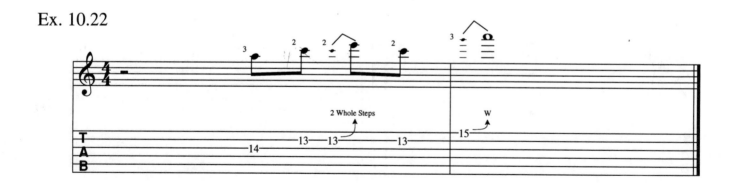

86

Ex. 10.23

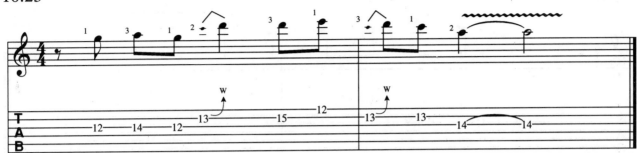

Ex. 10.24

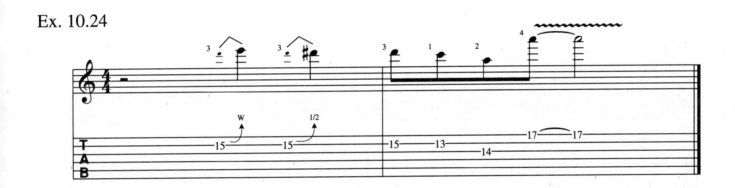

Ex. 10.25

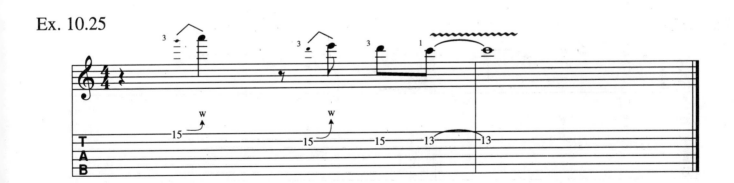

Ex. 10.26

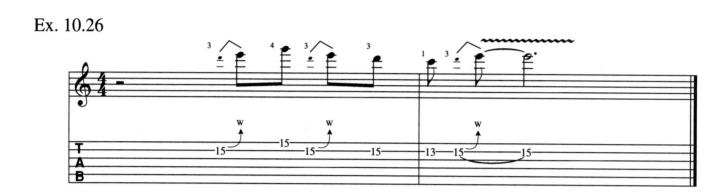

You can also bend using your first finger. Most first finger bends usually bend towards the ground.

Ex. 10.27

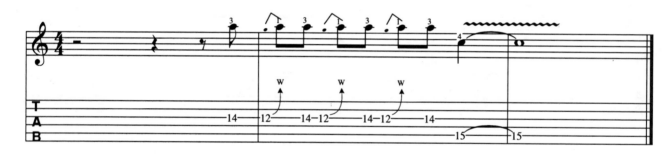

Ex. 10.28

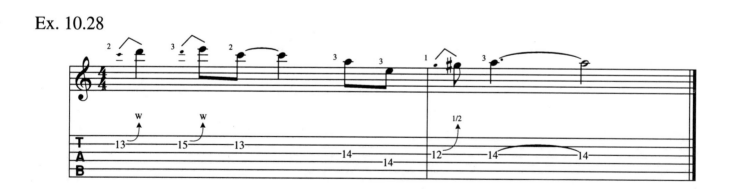

Ex. 10.29

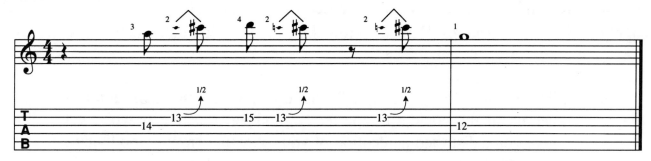

While there are many areas of rock guitar covered in this book, concentrate on one area at a time. This will make the material less overwhelming.

Everyone can create music. One of the most important aspects of rock guitar is being creative. Having a desire to create is the only requirement to creativity. Take what you can from this music and make it your own. In this next section we'll put the scales and techniques to work using the play-alongs.

Improvising

Improvisation means to make things up without any set preparation. Naturally, this would strike fear in anyone just starting. But, there is a certain amount of preparation when it comes to improvising. Throughout the book we have learned various scales, licks, and techniques which we can apply to our improvisations. Here are a few things to keep in mind when first starting out:

1. **The Basics** -Are you in tune? This might seem obvious to a lot of people but this could ruin a perfectly good performance, or worse yet give you a distorted perception of your playing. Are you too loud? I know "If it's too loud, you're too old" but you should try to blend in with the band. Be a team player, it will only make the group sound that much better.

2. **What is the key of the song?** - How to identify the roots of the scales you're playing.

3. **Think rhythmically** - How you phrase your notes. Are you playing too much? Remember, you're telling a story with your solo's.

4. **Have Fun** – So what if you hit some bad notes it's not the end of the world. I'm sure you'll also surprise yourself as well with the things you play.

After playing for a while this process should start to feel pretty natural. What has evolved into the rock sound today, as we know it, has to do with players improvising on what others have already done. Push yourself into different areas you might not have otherwise explored. Improvising, it's what will keep your playing fresh.

Improvising Vs. Pre -Planned Solos

Pre-planned or already constructed solos certainly have their place in rock music. Many rock bands will go for a more structured sound with an emphasis on songs rather than improvising. If you're not playing in your Phish or Grateful Dead tribute band this weekend, maybe it's best to keep your improv to a minimum. It all depends on what type of musical setting you're in. The Eagles "Hotel California," Randy Rhoads "Crazy Train" to David Gilmore's solo on Pink Floyd's "Money" are classic solos that are just as much a part of the song as the melody and chord progressions. It would take away from the song if they were altered in any way. These solos definitely came about from improvising and then constructing a solo from that. If there is a hook that is essential to the song by all means, you should play it. So which should you do? Many players will shift between improvising and pre planned solos. There is no right or wrong way to play - just options.

Play Alongs

Finally, here are four play along tracks to get you actually applying the ideas and techniques you have learned. The four tunes are all based on the twelve bar blues progression put into various styles. The blues progression has been used in every area of rock music. When first getting ready to play listen to the tune first. How fast or slow is it and most important what key is it in.

#70

Eddie from Etna

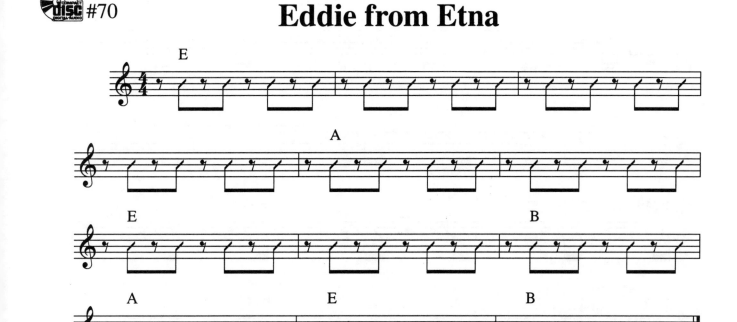

Deli Boy Blues

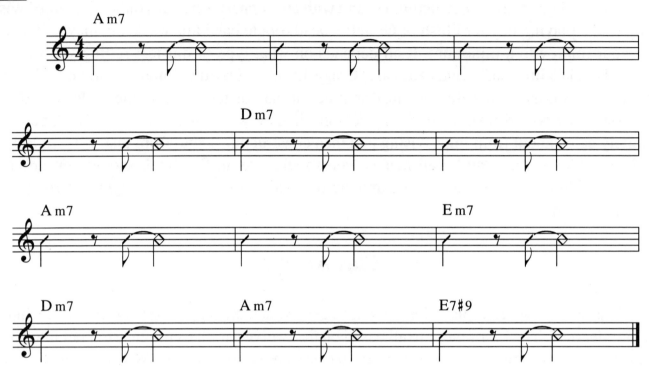

Funktion

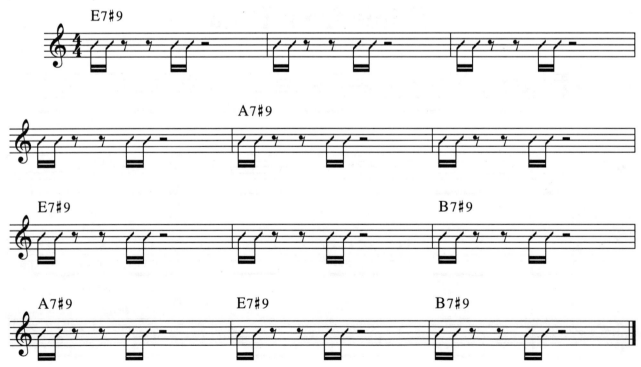

"Riff Raff" demonstrates how you can use riffs to create this Zeppelinesque type groove. Again, you can use the E minor pentatonic to improvise with.

Riff Raff

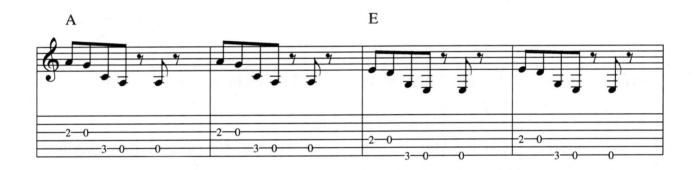

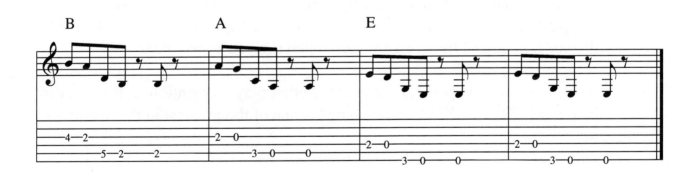

Suggested Listening

If you've recently gotten into rock you might need a little direction on what to listen to other than the mainstream. There are many different areas of rock. Taking ideas from one or all will be quite beneficial in your musical development. Here are a few of my personal favorites. Ask any rock player and I'm sure they'll agree with me.

The Classics

• Jeff Beck - Blow by Blow-"Cause We Ended As Lovers."

• Eric Clapton- Clapton has always been a great guitarist hands down but my favorite is the Layla CD, plus you get Duane Allman for the same price of admission.

• Jimmy Page-"Since I've been Loving You" from Led Zeppelin III showcases some of Page's best blues playing.

• Robin Trower - once dismissed as a Hendrix wannabe, Trower; with his psychedelic blues infested playing, delivered a landmark album with "Bridge of Sighs."

• Van Halen's - "Fair Warning" and "Women and Children First" show some of Eddie's most unabandonded playing.

• Jimi Hendrix – "Castles Made of Sand" has some of his best rhythm playing. Check out the compilation CD "Blues" for some top notch Hendrix.

• Santana- Before the recent success of his self-titled comeback, Santana had been making great music for years. Check out the live version of "Europa" from Moonflower for some of the most emotional playing you'll ever hear.

• Larry Carlton – Not as popular as some of the other players mentioned, but Larry's solo from Steely Dan's "Kid Charlemagne" is one of the greatest in the history of rock.

Blues

• Stevie Ray Vaughan - what can I say that hasn't already been said about Stevie Ray. One of my favorites is "Lenny" from "Texas Flood."

• B.B. King- every guitarist should know "The Thrill is Gone"-it's a classic.

Blues with a Twist

- Scott Henderson - known primarily as a fusion monster, Scott has recently been putting his unique slant on the blues. Check out "Dog Party."

- Robben Ford - great phrasing and a killer tone "Talk to your Daughter" and "Robben Ford and the Blue Line" are some of his best.

Shredder Days Ahead

- Yngwie Malmsteen - Just how Eddie Van Halen changed the guitar world forever in the late 70's. 1984's Rising Force spawned the 80's shred era, Yngwie's best.

- Steve Vai - Talk about having a personality on the instrument, Vai is one of rock's most gifted guitarists ever to come on the scene. Vai has played with everyone from Frank Zappa to the David Lee Roth band (who else could fill Eddie's shoes).

Masters of the Riff

- Black Sabbath – have pretty much invented heavy metal. The CD "Paranoid" has produced such classic riffs as "Iron Man" and the title track. Plus my personal favorite "Electric Funeral."

Southern Rock

- Allman Brothers – the south has produced some of the most well rounded musicians. Jazz, Funk, Blues the Allmans have it all. "Live at the Fillmore East" is essential listening.

- Lynyrd Skynyrd - Three guitar players in the same band and they still manage not to step on each others toes. Do yourself a favor and check out "I Know A Little" for some great pick'n complements of Ed King. "Sweet Home Alabama" is also a must know for all rock guitarists.

- Warren Haynes - Warren has been breathing new life back into the jam band scene with his band Gov't. Mule.

Acknowledgements

This book is dedicated in memory of my grandfather and friend:

Stephen J. Delach

To my most supportive wife Jennifer, Mother Marlene, Dad and Lynn, Brothers Sean and Scott, the Vallecorsa, Cherico, Reissman families, Jerry Cygnarowicz, Steve "Weet" Larcovic, Corey Congillio, Doug Kasper, Bill Ferchak, Eddie Adams, Brad Johnson, Art Boehm, Frank Danyo, John Purse and all the guys at Lawrence Music.

Mark Koch and Ken Karsh, for being great teachers.

A very special thanks to Bill Purse and Duquesne University's Guitar department.

Thanks to the great players on the CD; Lou Ross on Drums and Jake Kish on Bass.

Most of all, I thank God for the talent bestowed upon me, and the gift to be able to give it back through teaching.